D1299419

TEEN MENTAL HEALTH™

divorce and
stepfamilies

Rosie L. Peterman,
Jared Meyer, and
Charlie Quill

ROSEN
PUBLISHING®

New York

Published in 2013 by The Rosen Publishing Group, Inc.
29 East 21st Street, New York, NY 10010

First Edition

Library of Congress Cataloging-in-Publication Data

Peterman, Rosie L.
Divorce and stepfamilies/Rosie L. Peterman, Jared Meyer,
Charlie Quill.—1st ed.
    p. cm.—(Teen mental health)
Includes bibliographical references and index.
ISBN 978-1-4488-6893-3 (library binding)
1. Stepfamilies—Juvenile literature. 2. Divorce—
Psychological aspects—Juvenile literature. 3. Children of
divorced parents—Juvenile literature. 4. Teenagers—
Juvenile literature. I. Meyer, Jared. II. Quill, Charlie. III. Title.
HQ759.92.P45 2013
306.89—dc23
                                                        2012001159

Manufactured in the United States of America

CPSIA Compliance Information: Batch #S12YA: For further information, contact Rosen Publishing, New York, New York,
at 1-800-237-9932.

contents

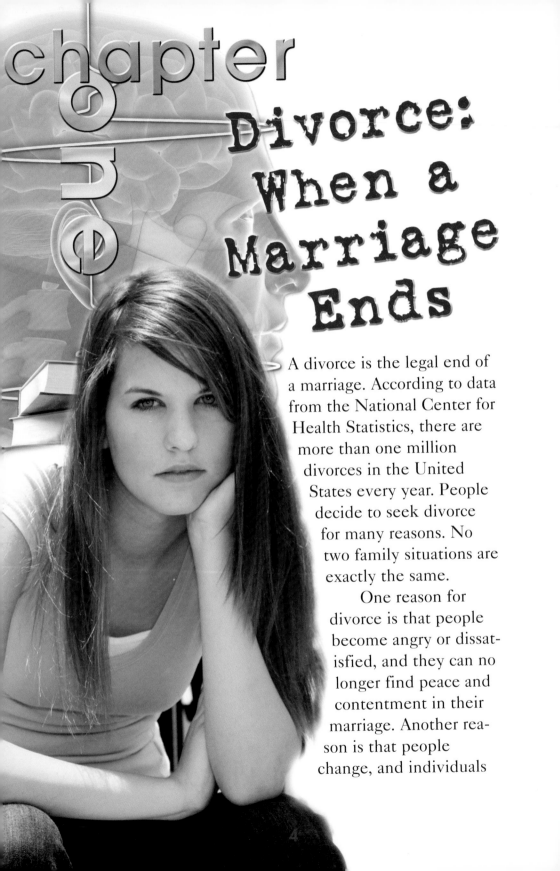

chapter one

Divorce: When a Marriage Ends

A divorce is the legal end of a marriage. According to data from the National Center for Health Statistics, there are more than one million divorces in the United States every year. People decide to seek divorce for many reasons. No two family situations are exactly the same.

One reason for divorce is that people become angry or dissatisfied, and they can no longer find peace and contentment in their marriage. Another reason is that people change, and individuals are sometimes unable to address or adjust to the changes. Whatever the reasons might be, divorce is a disruption of the familiar, normal flow of one's life, and it can be deeply unsettling and often very painful.

A Shocking Event

Divorce occurs often, and it can happen to anyone. In some families, the decision to separate can happen quite suddenly, leaving teenagers unprepared and causing shock and dismay. When divorce in their family happens

The end of a marriage can be stressful, frustrating, and upsetting. It is difficult to witness conflict in your parents' relationship.

suddenly, children and teens naturally wonder what will happen to them and whether their lives will ever be normal again.

Whether teens are somewhat prepared for their parents' divorce or are surprised by it when it is announced, they will all be deeply affected by what is happening in their families. A lot of us fear change, and divorce brings many changes. When news of a divorce arrives as a sudden announcement, it can be a profound shock to your emotions. It may produce a feeling of uncertainty and a lack of confidence and hope for the future.

You may have known that divorce happens to others but may not have thought it would ever affect you. You might wonder how your life could be turned upside down so quickly and why there does not seem to be anything you can do about it. Most of all, you may be wondering how and why this could happen.

A Host of Emotions

If your parents are in the process of separating or divorcing or have already divorced, it is normal for you to have a range of strong emotions, from anxiety to relief. There is no "right" way to feel about the situation. You might react to your situation in one way, but someone else might react in quite another. Over time, your feelings and ideas about the divorce will likely change, too.

Divorce is usually a painful experience for everyone. This includes the parents and the children. If you are suddenly living with only one parent, you may experience

When you first learn about your parents' divorce, you may find yourself worrying about everything, large and small. Be sure to get support so that you don't feel so alone.

sadness and a feeling of loss. You will naturally miss your absent parent. You may also be very angry with one or both of your parents. You may blame them for splitting up your family. Or, you may simply feel angry about the situation in general.

You may also feel some guilt about the divorce. Many children and teens think that they have somehow caused their parents' divorce. However, a husband and wife get a divorce because of their own problems, not because of

7

something the children have said or done. The children feel guilty about something that was beyond their control.

If you ever suspect that something you did caused your parents to divorce, tell your parents your thoughts. They can reassure you that their divorce was not your fault. A divorce is between a husband and wife—not between parents and their children.

Some teens see that their parents are clearly not getting along but still hold on to the hope that they will work out their differences. They resist the divorce. They may attempt to delay or stall the process in the hope that their parents will stay together.

Believe it or not, it is also normal for teens to feel relief at their parents' divorce announcement. It is extremely difficult for young people to witness long-term fighting and hostility between parents. A home should be a place of shelter, love, and security. These qualities may no longer be available to someone whose parents are getting along poorly. This can cause a great deal of stress for the entire family. Therefore, you may feel some relief as a result of your parents' decision to divorce.

All of these feelings are natural. And they will take time to get over. During a divorce you need to talk to your parents, siblings, or other trusted relatives and friends about your feelings and fears. Often, teens find it difficult to share their feelings openly, and you might also. Maybe you are too embarrassed or think no one will understand your feelings. However, telling others how you feel can really help. Talking with a counselor can also help you process your feelings.

Custody and Living Arrangements

With a divorce, there are many issues to settle, especially for teens. Besides the emotional trauma that accompanies divorce, there are practical issues that parents must resolve. One major issue is who will take care of the children, and where and with whom the children will live, once the parents separate.

Custody can be one of the most important (and contentious) issues in a breakup or divorce. Determining child custody is creating an agreement about how parenting responsibilities will be divided. When divorcing parents cannot agree over who will have responsibility for taking care of their teen, a judge in a court of law makes the decision for them. In making their decision, judges often try to determine what arrangement would be in the best interest of the teen.

Feeling stuck in the middle of custody decisions can be confusing and depressing. But if you know about the different types of custody and what they mean, then you can better understand and adjust to your new living situation.

Types of Custody

Commonly, there are two parts to each type of custody—legal and physical. Legal custody determines who will make decisions about a teen's education, health care, and other important issues, and physical custody determines with whom the child will live. Depending on the facts of a couple's case and state standards, there can be joint custody (shared custody) or sole custody (custody given to

Your parents may go to court to settle custody and visitation issues. In reaching their decisions, judges consider many factors, including the parents' physical and mental health, sibling relationships, and what the teen wants.

just one parent). If one parent is given sole custody, then generally the other has visitation rights—the legal right to visit and spend time with the child.

Sometimes parents can split up amicably, without fighting or feeling very angry. In this situation, they may agree to full joint custody. Parents agree to share both physical and legal custody of the child. There are many ways parents can share their time with you. For example, you might live with your father during half the week and stay with your mother for the other half. Both parents will make decisions about your welfare and share general parenting responsibilities.

Parents can also decide to share joint legal custody but have one parent maintain sole physical custody. While you may live with one parent, your parents will, whenever possible, consult with each other when it comes to making important decisions about you, such as choices about education, religious upbringing, and health care. This means, for example, that one parent can't decide to change your school without seeking input from the other. With joint legal custody, both parents have an equal say regarding your welfare, no matter which parent you spend more time with.

Splitting Your Time

How you will split up your time between parents is determined by a number of factors, including where your parents live. For example, if your parents live in the same school district or neighborhood, you may be able to switch locations often, with less disruption to your routine. Parents with more distance between them may make alternative arrangements to share your time, perhaps alternating months or weeks.

In many cases, teens alternate where they spend holidays. One year, your father may take you to see his family for Thanksgiving, and the next year you might be with your mother's relatives. School and summer vacations can also be arranged this way. It is very important that all family members are aware of the schedule and that plans are made far enough in advance to give everyone time to adjust to any changes.

There are even products on the market designed to make shared custodial arrangements flow more smoothly. Computer tools can help parents coordinate schedules with an online calendar that is easily accessible to both. Any time a parent wants to alter the schedule, he or she can just e-mail the other parent the proposed change and then have it reflected online. This is particularly helpful for parents who have difficulty communicating with each other in person.

What if your parents are fighting about custody? Do you have to take sides? Emotionally, it may be difficult not to. However, it is rare that a teenager, especially a younger teen, would be made to testify in court about which parent he or she would prefer to live with. What is more likely to happen is that a professional assigned by the court—usually a psychologist, therapist, or social worker—will interview the teen about his or her home life and feelings about the situation and then issue a report to the court. The judge may or may not make a decision about custody based on the recommendations in such a report.

chapter TWO
Adjusting to Life After Divorce

Teens that go through a divorce often find their worlds turned upside down. A divorce changes more than your home situation. It can also affect your family's finances, what city or town you live in, and where you go to school. All of these can be drastic changes, and they often happen in a very short time.

If your family is going through a divorce, there will be a lot to get used to. You may have to adjust to many new things: a new relationship with your parents, new friends, and a new community, for instance. Though you may stay in the same home, there is the chance that you will move. You may have to move away from old friends and find ways to maintain those friendships. You will also be learning to adjust to new relationships in your parents' lives.

Change is often hard to deal with. Over time, though, you will become more comfortable with your new situation.

Living in Multiple Homes

The idea of living in two different houses can seem awkward, sad, and uncomfortable at first, but once a pattern is established, it can work out, and you can still be close with each member of your family. This kind of arrangement keeps both of your parents actively involved in your upbringing.

Adjusting to your new home life takes time. Living in two homes means you'll need to create personal space at each. It can help to surround yourself with physical comforts and try to make both homes as much yours as possible. This includes decorating two different bedrooms and keeping all necessary supplies—clothes, toothbrushes, books, and music—at each home. Even though keeping all the necessities and comforts at two homes might result in duplicating things, having what you need can help you feel more "at home" when living in each place.

Another adjustment you might have to make is learning the rules at each household. When parents live together, they generally agree upon one set of rules; however, when they each set up house, they may very well have different rules and expectations. It's important to know what is expected, as well as tolerated, in each home. Unfortunately, you will probably have to follow these rules even if you do not agree with them.

A New Community

Your parents' divorce may mean that you have to move away from the area where you have lived. This change in your life will have an impact on your friendships. When divorce necessitates a move to another town or city, it means that you will be saying good-bye to old friends. However, this does not necessarily mean that you have to say good-bye to the friendships. You may be seeing each other on your visits with one of your parents, and you can communicate by mail, e-mail, or telephone. If your friends are important to you, you can find ways to stay in touch with them and exchange news about what is going on in each of your worlds.

In some cases, it may be necessary to move and go to a new school. If this happens, you can use technology to stay in touch with friends from your old school.

15

Missing Your Other Parent

One of the hardest things to get used to after divorce is the new order of your life. All of a sudden you can't see both of your parents every day. You also may see one of your parents less often than the other.

Usually, though, you will still be able to see your other parent regularly. Your parent may visit you often, or you may spend weekends with him or her. It can help to keep in touch between visits by phone, e-mail, or video chat. That way, he or she can stay up-to-date on your daily life. Another thing you can do is keep a picture of your parent at the other parent's home.

When you are together, talk to your parent about how sad the divorce has made you feel. Explain that you still love and miss him or her. Communicating in this way may allow your parent to open up as well. Your parent will likely reassure you that he or she misses you, too, and wants to continue to be an important part of your life.

New Relationships with Parents

Your parents' custody arrangement may separate you physically from one of your parents. However, the separation does not necessarily have to interfere with the parental influence that your parent has in your development. That parent might, in fact, become an even stronger influence in your life. You and your parent may learn to place a greater value on the time you have together.

It may take added effort on the part of your parent and you to develop and maintain this closeness, but the

Even if your parents are divorced, you can still enjoy the support, guidance, and love of each parent.

effort is worth it. When this happens, you may begin to seek the guidance and advice of your parent in positive ways. Keep in mind that some teens use one parent to challenge the advice or directions of the other. This is a negative way to respond to your situation and can prolong the adjustment period.

New Independence and Responsibilities

After the divorce, you will probably have more time alone, without either of your parents. A single parent will have a

17

little less time, perhaps, to spread between work, home, and parental responsibilities. Your custodial parent may be working longer hours, or just starting to work. Your mother or father's longer hours away from home may require you to develop a more responsible attitude and become more independent. You may have to help out more around the house. You may have to do household chores or help take care of younger brothers or sisters.

Sometimes, this change in responsibility causes negative emotions, like anger, sadness, rebellious feelings, or wanting to withdraw. Discuss these emotions with your parent, and then work with him or her to come up with a manageable way for you to be supported with your new responsibilities.

Parents That Date

Adjusting to your new family arrangement is a challenge in itself, but you may also be faced with an even bigger challenge—your parents starting to date new people. If your parents do start to date, or perhaps even decide to remarry, you may face many different emotional challenges.

First, it is natural to feel protective of your parent and your relationship with him or her. You may also look for comparisons between a new individual and your other parent. Also, spending time with your parent's dating partner may place you in an uncomfortable middle position. One parent might question you about the activities of the other parent. Hopefully, your parents will avoid doing this, as it can place more of a burden on you as you struggle with this new life. In time, you will learn to adjust to your parents' new relationships.

Getting Support

When you are in the middle of the messiness of your parents' separation and divorce, you will have many complicated emotions. But there are ways that you can gain a better understanding of these feelings. During this time, you need support.

A counselor or therapist can help you if you are having difficulty with your parents' divorce or just need a sounding board outside your family.

The first step toward healing is to seek understanding of your situation. You will need help with this; you cannot do it alone. Sometimes this help can come directly from your parents. However, in the early stages of their separation and divorce, they may be too overwhelmed and unable to help you as much as you need. This is the time to seek other resources. If you need to talk to someone to get advice, you can start by talking to your counselor at school. If he or she feels you need to talk to someone else, such as a psychologist or social worker, he or she can refer you.

There are also a lot of books, both fiction and nonfiction, that deal with all of the things you might experience during this time. Reading can give you a greater understanding of the complexities of divorce and perhaps offer some insight into how your parents might feel.

No one expects separation and divorce to be an easy time, particularly for teens, so you shouldn't feel strange looking for a little information, support, or advice. In the end, it could make the transition to a new way of family life easier for everyone.

MYTHS AND FACTS

Myth: Teens are sometimes partially or entirely the reason for their parents' divorce.

Fact: A teen's behavior is never the specific cause of his or her parents' divorce. Adults get divorced because their relationship is irreparable based on their chemistry, compatibility, communication styles, and long-term life goals. Divorce can also be caused by problems such as economic stress, substance abuse, interpersonal abuse, or infidelity.

Myth: People who have failed marriages are considered to be "damaged goods" or to have "lots of baggage."

Fact: While divorce has different stereotypes and some people do leave marriages with internal conflict and mental suffering, many go on to begin new and healthy relationships, often with others who also were once married.

Myth: All Americans have a 50 percent chance of getting divorced.

Fact: According to research reported by David Popenoe and Barbara Dafoe Whitehead at Rutgers University, although the overall divorce rate in America is close to 50 percent of all marriages, for large segments of the population, the risk of divorce is far below 50 percent. The risk of divorce is lower for people who have a college degree or higher and are entering their first marriage. It is also lower for people who wait to marry until their mid-twenties or later and for religious people who marry someone of the same faith.

chapter three

Stepfamilies: When a Parent Remarries

According to the National Stepfamily Resource Center, about 75 percent of divorced people remarry, making it fairly likely that if your parents are divorced, one or both of them will get married again. According to the same organization, about 65 percent of second marriages involve children from previous marriages.

When a parent remarries after a divorce or the death of a spouse, a stepfamily, also known as a blended family, is formed. The new spouse is a stepparent (a stepmother or a stepfather) to the

Blended families are formed when remarriages occur and children share only one or no biological parents.

children from the parent's first marriage. Stepfamilies can also include siblings, stepsiblings, and half siblings.

Stepfamilies are common today. Perhaps you are a member of one of them, or even two of them if both of your biological parents have remarried. According to the U.S. Census Bureau, in 2009, 5.6 million children lived with at least one stepparent. Also, a Pew Research Center survey reported that 42 percent of American adults today have at least one step relative in their family—a stepparent, a stepsibling or half sibling, or a stepchild.

A New Marriage

If you learn that one of your parents is getting remarried, you may have many different emotions. You may be upset that your parent is marrying someone other than your mother or father. You may be angry, believing that your parent's new spouse will try to take the place of your absent parent. Perhaps you fear that your stepparent will ruin the special relationship you have with your natural parent.

Many teens have difficulty when a parent announces remarriage because it is a sign that the romantic relationship between their parents is truly over. Even if your parents' divorce was finalized, you may have hoped that they would get back together someday. This is a rare event, however. Trying to accept the situation and move on is the best way to handle it.

This does not mean that it will be easy to adjust to your parent's remarriage. It will likely take a lot of courage, a lot of work, and a lot of time. As a result, this difficult time may be the most important period of growth that you will experience in your life.

A New Family

Learning to be part of a stepfamily is often a challenge. As a teenager, it may be especially difficult to adjust to the complexities of stepfamily life. You are already going through the many transitions of adolescence, including gaining more independence and seeking your own identity. These changes are complicated by having to adapt to the dynamics of a new family.

With the formation of new family units, stepparents and stepsiblings may play new roles in your life. You may have a variety of emotions and concerns regarding your new family. You may feel sad or angry, or you may be excited about the new situation. You may be wondering where you will fit in.

If you are living with the blended family, your daily life might change. You may have to share a room with a stepsibling. You may be anxious about your stepparent living in the same house. Will you still be able to spend time alone with your biological parent? Who will make the rules? Many questions like these may arise during the formation of the new family.

On the other hand, you may have positive feelings about the remarriage. Your stepsiblings and stepparent may become great companions. They may become new friends in your life. Even though remarriage is a big change, it doesn't have to be a bad thing.

Not Always Wicked: Getting Beyond Stereotypes

You probably remember the fairy tales Snow White and the Seven Dwarfs and Cinderella from childhood. In both stories, the main character had a wicked stepmother: a cold and heartless woman, jealous of her stepdaughter's charm and beauty. Cinderella's stepmother punished her by forcing her to perform incessant household duties and forbidding her to leave the house. Her evil stepsisters taunted her.

The characters in these stories have helped to create negative stereotypes of stepfamilies in our society. As a result of your exposure to these scary images, you may have a negative perception of how your stepfamily will work.

It is important to understand that the images from these fairy tales are fictional and not always accurate. Just because your parent is getting remarried does not mean that your stepparent will take an instant dislike to you. The fact that you are an important person in your parent's life will make you an important person in your stepparent's life. Because of that, he or she will likely want to develop a good relationship with you.

Stepsiblings

Just as your stepparent will play an important role in your life, so will your stepsiblings. You may end up sharing a room with a stepsibling, putting you in very close quarters. Adolescence can be a tough time in life to start living with brand-new people, particularly if other teens are involved. As a teenager, the last thing you may want is to deal with somebody

While you may worry at first about living with stepsiblings, in time you'll become more comfortable cooperating in everyday situations.

else's changes, confusion, or mood swings. You may feel you have enough to handle in your own life.

Still, try to consider your stepsiblings as positive additions to your family. A stepsibling is in a similar situation to yours and is also trying to fit into a new, blended family. In fact, a stepsibling can simply be a friend. If you are close in age, this is even more likely to happen. You might be surprised to find that it is nice to have a stepsibling around—a peer you can talk to—either in addition to your natural siblings or as a sibling you never had.

You may experience big changes in a stepfamily, including gaining a new half sibling.

Half Siblings

At some point, your blended family may expand even more if your parent and stepparent decide to have a child together. Since you have one common biological parent, this child will be your half sibling.

A baby causes many lifestyle changes for parents and families. Having a new baby enter the family may also stir up many emotions. You may feel jealous of all the attention the baby gets. In addition, the baby may be a strong reminder of the existence of your stepfamily and the fact that your natural parents are not together anymore. However, the baby is your half brother or half sister, a bond that cannot be broken or ignored.

Although from a teenage perspective, it may be hard to identify with a new child, try to understand the baby's needs and think of him or her in a positive way. If your parent and stepparent ask you to help take care of the baby or perform other chores, be flattered. It means that you are independent and responsible enough to be trusted with your new brother or sister, as well as with other jobs that will make daily life in your household run more smoothly. It is a big step toward adulthood.

Connection Versus Independence

As an adolescent, you are likely experiencing many changes in your life. Aside from the physical changes of growth, you are also encountering psychological changes. At this point in life, you begin to separate from your family and develop a strong individual identity. You may have only a few years or so before you go off to college or get a job, move out of your house, and become more independent. These possibilities may make it even harder to focus on being a part of your stepfamily. However, just as you are moving toward these personal transitions, you are simultaneously expected to join this new family group and are depended upon to help make it work. It is a challenge, but you can do both. You can still be your own person while also being an integral part of your stepfamily.

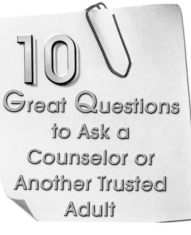

10 Great Questions to Ask a Counselor or Another Trusted Adult

1. How can I deal with my sadness and anger about my parents' divorce?

2. What is the best way that all of us can move on with the least amount of conflict or drama?

3. How can I handle having a different set of house rules in each of my parent's homes?

4. I'll be living in two homes. How can I best organize my clothing, books, school supplies, and other items so I will have what I need?

5. How will my parents' breakup affect my life compared to my friends whose parents are still together?

6. What can I do to develop a positive relationship with my stepparent and stepsiblings?

7. What can I do to maintain my privacy now that I'll be sharing a home with more people than in the past?

8. What will it be like if and when I have a new half sibling?

9. What should I do if my other parent becomes jealous of my stepparent?

10. Will my parents' divorce affect my own success with relationships and marriage?

chapter four

Adjusting to Life in a Stepfamily

One of the most difficult challenges members of stepfamilies face is dealing with change. Your stepfamily life may be drastically different from your life before your parent remarried. It is to your benefit to try to cope with the changes in a positive way.

There are a variety of things you can do to adjust to stepfamily life, different people with whom you can talk about your worries and fears, and various strategies for dealing with your feelings. You can work

Participating in enjoyable family activities, such as game nights, can help everyone adjust to stepfamily life.

your way through the transition with the help of your family or those outside the family, such as friends or counselors.

Adjusting to Change

Getting used to stepfamily life involves adjusting to many changes. For example, you may be asked to take on new roles and responsibilities in your stepfamily. Whereas before you used to walk the dog and take out the garbage, your responsibilities may now include helping prepare meals or doing the dishes instead.

31

You may also have to adjust to some of the different characteristics of your new family members. Perhaps you are quiet and shy, whereas your new stepparent and stepsiblings are more outgoing. Learning to accept other people's differences is something you will all need to do in order to help make the blended family work.

Getting involved in family activities can be helpful in your adjustment. If you are indeed shy and have trouble handling group situations, this may be challenging at first and take some time. Also, as a teen working toward greater independence, it is normal for you to want to spend more time by yourself and with your friends. However, if you are withdrawing from your stepfamily because you are angry about your parent's remarriage, you may only be making your situation worse. You may be letting your resentment prevent you from making the best of things, and you may find yourself more excluded and isolated. You may also be missing out on what could be a fun, enjoyable family situation. The more involved you are with the family, the more comfortable you may begin to feel in the group and the more you may fit in.

Making the Stepfamily Work

It takes a lot of effort on everybody's part to make a stepfamily work. Once all the members of the family come to terms with the situation and begin to work together as one unit, the blended family can be considered a real family, not a forced unification.

There are several things that members of a step-family can do to help them through the rough spots of creating their family dynamic. One of these things is to identify what family members have in common. The people in blended families have all experienced losses. If your parents have divorced, you may feel great sadness about it, and you may think that nobody can understand what you are going through. However, if you now have stepsiblings who also went through divorce, try talking to them about your experiences. You may be surprised to find that they are probably feeling the same emotions of grief and anger, and talking about it with one another can help you feel less alone.

Stepfamilies must also develop new skills and learn how to make decisions as a group. Family meetings are a good way to get to know each other and to talk about each person's feelings and needs. You may be surprised at how getting together to talk about fears, anxieties, and hopes can prove to be quite helpful.

Family members must also be open to change and compromise. Try to accept new ideas and ways of doing things that differ from the ways you used to do them. Give new ideas a chance before you dismiss them. One of the biggest obstacles blended families face is that they lack a shared family history or shared ways of doing things, and they may have different beliefs. If you can try to be open to new circumstances and responsibilities within the family, new traditions will arise.

Feelings Toward Your Stepparent

One-on-one time with your mother or father can reassure you that your parent continues to share a special bond with you.

As you begin to deal with your new stepparent and his or her role in your life, it is natural to experience some negative feelings or resentment. It is difficult enough to come to terms with the fact that one parent no longer lives in your house; coping with a new person in a parental role may not be easy. You may also resent the fact that your mother or father now relies upon a new spouse for help and support, whereas before your parent may have relied upon you. It is as though the responsibilities you took on are no longer needed. This is especially common in the case of an only child. Often, a unique bond exists between the parent and child because it is just the two of them together after a divorce or separation.

Even while trying to adjust to your stepfamily, there might often be a need for you to spend time alone with your biological parent. Having special time alone with your parent will help you in your adjustment to the blended family. It will provide an outlet for you to speak privately with your parent and express any feelings and anxieties you may be having. In addition, this time together can be an assurance that you have not lost your parent during the formation of the stepfamily. Spending time alone together will allow you and your parent to have a little time out just to enjoy being together, and it will reassure you that your parent is still there for you.

Parental Hurt and Anger

After divorce, some people harbor negative feelings toward their ex-spouses. Unfortunately, some parents deal with these feelings in unhealthy ways, by starting arguments or spewing destructive criticism. The parents may bad-mouth each other in front of their children, and they may also criticize a stepparent. It may be hard for the parents to put the children's needs ahead of their own anger and resentment toward each other. They unfairly put the children in the middle.

If you are in this situation, do not be afraid to talk to your parents when they make comments about your other parent or stepparent that make you upset. Often, if parents learn how much this behavior is bothering you, they may realize that they are making an already rough situation even worse.

You may also feel confused if you like your stepparent and begin to develop a relationship with him or her. You may feel that you are hurting your absent parent by being friendly with this new person. You may even feel disloyal. It is similar to the feeling you may have experienced after your parents divorced: while spending time with one parent, you may have felt disloyal to the other.

It is important for you to realize that it is OK to like your stepparent, and you don't need to feel guilty or disloyal. As you continue to grow and mature, you may even realize that by getting along with your stepparent, you have helped create a more harmonious family. Ultimately, this will have a positive influence on your and others' well-being.

Talk About It

Like many teens in your situation, you may find it helpful to talk to an outside professional who can help guide you through the tough issues you are facing. There are many people who can help you, such as school psychologists, social workers, and religious leaders. You may be surprised at how a fresh set of eyes can make a situation a little clearer.

Another outlet that can be a great help in coping is a support group for teens. A support group helps people deal with an issue that has affected their lives, such as divorce or the death of a family member. You may find one right in your own school, run by a teacher or a school social worker. An example is the Banana Splits program for children of divorce, found in many schools around the country. You may also find support groups in community centers or at the office of a counselor or psychologist.

A support group can be helpful for several reasons. First, it is often easier to talk about problems in a group

In a support group, you can process your feelings with other teens who have gone through similar experiences. Topics discussed are typically kept confidential.

setting where everyone has experienced similar life changes and can identify with your feelings. In a group that focuses on divorce and stepfamilies, you may find it useful to hear other teens' stories and strategies for coping. It may give you some ideas on how to adjust to your own situation. The group can also be a good outlet through which to express your anger, sadness, or whatever you are feeling to people who will listen and sympathize.

Family Counseling

In cases where families can't seem to get along, the help of a family counselor may be necessary. A family counselor may talk to family members individually. He or she may also invite the entire family to counseling sessions to talk out any problems. Having an objective listener can be a great asset. The counselor can lend an unbiased ear and provide suggestions and solutions for solving problems after listening to what each person has to say.

Counselors can also act as intermediaries between family members who are having a dispute. They may be more successful in helping the family assess the situation and try to solve it than if the family members continue to battle it out at home. This can be very helpful if there are multiple children in the family, as they often have the hardest time in their adjustment.

It can be beneficial to continue going to the counseling sessions over an extended period of time. This way, the counselor becomes the family's friend and adviser and has the chance to watch the family dynamic develop and improve with time. After a while, the counselor will be able to assess the progress that has been made and advise the family members on how to continue working together and solving their problems.

Although forming a stepfamily can be extremely difficult in a variety of ways, it does not have to be an altogether negative experience. Although they are not the same as first-married families, stepfamilies can be wonderful, too. Living in a stepfamily takes work. However, if you make the effort and the other family members do as well, your stepfamily can be a positive part of your life.

adolescence The time of development between puberty and adulthood; the teenage years.

amicably In a peaceful or friendly manner.

child custody A court's determination about which parent or relative should have physical and/or legal control and responsibility for a child under age eighteen.

contentious Likely to cause argument or disagreement.

divorce The legal termination of a marriage.

ex-spouse A person who was formerly a spouse.

half sibling The child of one's biological parent and stepparent.

infidelity Unfaithfulness to one's husband or wife.

integral Needed for the completeness of the whole.

intermediary A person who acts as a go-between or mediator, working with opposing sides in an argument in order to bring about an agreement.

irreparable Not capable of being repaired.

joint custody A decision by a court, often upon agreement of the parents, that the parents will share custody (legal, physical, or both) of a child.

legal custody The legal right to make major decisions, such as those regarding education, religion, and health care, for a child under the age of eighteen. Legal custody can be sole or joint.

partner A counterpart in a marriage or an intimate relationship.

physical custody The physical care and supervision of a child under the age of eighteen, including providing the child's residence and living with the child. Physical custody can be sole or joint.

resentment An ongoing feeling of anger, bitterness, or ill will.

sole custody A decision by a court that only one parent has custody (legal, physical, or both) of a child.

spouse A person's partner in marriage; a husband or wife.

stepfamily A family that forms when two adults get married and at least one of them has a child or children from a previous marriage; also known as a blended family.

stepparent The spouse of one's parent by a subsequent marriage; a stepmother or stepfather.

stepsibling A stepbrother or a stepsister.

support group A group of people, sometimes led by a counselor or therapist, who provide each other with support, information, and advice on issues relating to a shared experience, such as divorce.

visitation The time that a parent without custody spends with his or her children; the parent's legal right to this time.

American Academy of Child and Adolescent Psychiatry
(AACAP)
3615 Wisconsin Avenue NW
Washington, DC 20016-3007
(202) 966-7300
Web site: http://www.aacap.org
The AACAP is a professional organization of psychiatrists
trained to promote healthy development and to eval-
uate, diagnose, and treat children and adolescents
who are affected by mental health issues. The organization publishes *Facts for Families* to provide
concise, up-to-date information on issues affecting
children, teens, and their families.

American Association for Marriage and Family Therapy
(AAMFT)
112 South Alfred Street
Alexandria, VA 22314
(703) 838-9808
Web site: http://www.aamft.org
The AAMFT is a professional association for the field of
marriage and family therapy. Since its founding in
1942, the AAMFT has been involved with the problems, needs, and changing patterns of couple and
family relationships.

Children's Rights Council (CRC)
9470 Annapolis Road, Suite 310
Lanham, MD 20706
(301) 459-1220
Web site: http://www.crckids.org

The CRC is a national nonprofit organization that deals
with custody issues and divorce reform and works to
ensure meaningful and continuing contact for children with both parents and extended families.

Dibble Institute
P.O. Box 7881
Berkeley, CA 94707-0881
(800) 695-7975
Web site: http://www.dibbleinstitute.org
The Dibble Institute is an independent, not-for-profit
organization that equips young people with the skills
and knowledge they need to develop healthy romantic relationships now and in the future.

Kids' Turn
55 New Montgomery Street, Suite 500
San Francisco, CA 94105
(415) 777-9977
Web site: http://www.kidsturn.org
This nonprofit organization provides educational programming for children and family members who are
affected by familial separation. It offers workshops
and resources for children, adolescents, and parents
experiencing separation or divorce.

National Marriage Project (NMP)
University of Virginia
P.O. Box 400766
Charlottesville, VA 22904-4766
(434) 982-4509

Web site: http://www.stateofourunions.org

The NMP is a nonpartisan, nonsectarian, and inter-disciplinary initiative located at the University of Virginia. The project's mission is to provide research and analysis on the health of marriage in America, to analyze the social and cultural forces shaping contemporary marriage, and to identify strategies to increase marital quality and stability.

National Stepfamily Resource Center
c/o Department of Human Development and Family Studies
203 Spidle Hall
Auburn University
Auburn, AL 36849
Web site: http://www.stepfamilies.info

The National Stepfamily Resource Center serves as a clearinghouse of information, linking family science research on stepfamilies and best practices in work with stepfamilies. Resources include facts and FAQs about stepfamilies, summaries of stepfamily research, and training institutes for therapists, counselors, and family life and marriage educators.

Rainbows Canada
80 Bradford Street, Suite 545
Barrie, ON L4N 6S7
Canada
(877) 403-2733
Web site: http://www.rainbows.ca/index.htm

Rainbows Canada is an international not-for-profit organization that fosters emotional healing among children and youth grieving a loss. These losses, among others, include separation, divorce, death, incarceration, foster care, and a military family member.

StepFamily Foundation of Alberta
4803 Centre Street Northwest, Suite 201
Calgary, AB T2E 2Z6
Canada
(403) 245-5744
Web site: http://www.stepfamily.ca
The Stepfamily Foundation of Alberta is a not-for-profit based in Calgary, Alberta, that focuses exclusively upon the concerns and needs of stepfamilies. The organization provides a variety of resources to help stepfamilies address and resolve the difficulties that are characteristic of the stepfamily experience.

Web Sites

Due to the changing nature of Internet links, Rosen Publishing has developed an online list of Web sites related to the subject of this book. This site is updated regularly. Please use this link to access the list:

http://www.rosenlinks.com/tmh/div

Buscemi, Karen. *Split in Two: Keeping It Together When Your Parents Live Apart.* San Francisco, CA: Zest Books, 2009.

Dessen, Sarah. *Along for the Ride: A Novel.* New York, NY: Viking, 2009.

Kiesbye, Stefan. *Blended Families* (Social Issues Firsthand). Detroit, MI: Greenhaven Press, 2009.

Mattern, Joanne. *Divorce* (The Real Deal). Chicago, IL: Heinemann Library, 2009.

Reinhardt, Dana. *How to Build a House.* New York, NY: Wendy Lamb Books, 2008.

Schab, Lisa M. *The Divorce Workbook for Teens: Activities to Help You Move Beyond the Breakup.* Oakland, CA: Instant Help Books, 2008.

Sewell, Earl. *Keysha's Drama.* New York, NY: Kimani Press, 2007.

Simons, Rae. *Blended Families* (Changing Face of Modern Families). Broomall, PA: Mason Crest Publishers, 2010.

Sindell, Max. *The Bright Side: Surviving Your Parents' Divorce.* Deerfield Beach, FL: Health Communications, 2007.

Stern, Zoe, Evan Stern, and Ellen Sue Stern. *Divorce Is Not the End of the World: Zoe and Evan's Coping Guide for Kids.* Rev. ed. Berkeley, CA: Tricycle Press, 2008.

Trueit, Trudi Strain. *Surviving Divorce: Teens Talk About What Hurts and What Helps* (Choices). New York, NY: Franklin Watts, 2007.

Winchester, Elizabeth. *Sisters and Brothers: The Ultimate Guide to Understanding Your Siblings and Yourself* (Choices). New York, NY: Franklin Watts, 2008.

Index

About the Author

Rosie L. Peterman writes for young adults and works professionally with teens in the social work field.

Jared Meyer is an author and speaker who helps people improve their decision-making and communication skills. In addition to writing books for young adults, he works as a marketing professional.

Charlie Quill is an author and journalist from Buffalo, New York. He has written several books that address mental health issues.

Photo Credits

Cover, pp. 1, 30 (couple) © istockphoto.com/Svetlana Braun; cover insets, p. 1 (top) Hemera/Thinkstock; (middle) © istockphoto.com/Jaimie Duplass; (bottom) © istockphoto.com/digitalskillet; pp. 1, 3, back cover (head and brain) © istockphoto.com/Vasiliy Yakobchuk; p. 3 (laptop) istockphoto.com/Doug De Suza; p. 4 © istockphoto.com/Steve Debenport; p. 5 Shutterstock/ejwhite.com; p. 7 Shutterstock/Diego Cervo; p. 10 © Rudi Von Briel/PhotoEdit; p. 13 © istockphoto.com/drbimages; p. 15 Ingram Publishing/Thinkstock; p. 17 Shutterstock/CREATISTA; p. 19 © istockphoto.com/Richard Clark; p. 22 © istockphoto.com/Juan Estey; p. 23 © Kayte Deioma/PhotoEdit; pp. 26, 31 © David Young-Wolfe/PhotoEdit; p 27 © Michael Newman/PhotoEdit; p. 34 Steve Mason/Photodisc/Thinkstock; p. 37 © Mary Kate Denny/PhotoEdit; interior graphics (books) © istockphoto.com/Michal Koziarski.

Designer: Nicole Russo; Editor: Andrea Sclarow Paskoff;
Photo Researcher: Marty Levick